# DRIVEABILITY DIAGNOSTICS

## NATEF Standards Lab Manual—AT 104

Jack Erjavec/Jim Clarke

**Vice President, Technology and Trades SBU:**
Alar Elken

**Editorial Director:**
Sandy Clark

**Senior Acquisitions Editor:**
David Boelio

**Development Editor:**
Christopher Shortt

**Marketing Director:**
Dave Garza

**Channel Manager:**
Bill Lawrensen

**Marketing Coordinator:**
Mark Pierro

**Production Director:**
Mary Ellen Black

**Production Manager:**
Larry Main

**Production Coordinator:**
Dawn Jacobson

**Project Editor:**
Toni Hansen

**Art-Design Specialist**
Rachel Baker

**Editorial Assistant:**
Kevin Rivenburg

COPYRIGHT © 2005 Thomson Delmar Learning. Thomson, the Star Logo, and Delmar Learning are trademarks used herein under license.

Printed in Canada
5 6 7  08 07 06

For more information contact
Thomson Delmar Learning
Executive Woods
5 Maxwell Drive, PO Box 8007,
Clifton Park, NY  12065-8007
Or find us on the World Wide Web at
www.delmarlearning.com

ALL RIGHTS RESERVED. No part of this work covered by the copyright hereon may be reproduced in any form or by any means—graphic, electronic, or mechanical, including photocopying, recording, taping, Web distribution, or information storage and retrieval systems—without the written permission of the publisher.

For permission to use material from the text or product, contact us by
Tel.      (800) 730-2214
Fax      (800) 730-2215
www.thomsonrights.com

Library of Congress Cataloging-in-Publication Data:
Card Number:

ISBN: 1-4018-8114-9

## NOTICE TO THE READER

Publisher does not warrant or guarantee any of the products described herein or perform any independent analysis in connection with any of the product information contained herein. Publisher does not assume, and expressly disclaims, any obligation to obtain and include information other than that provided to it by the manufacturer.

The reader is expressly warned to consider and adopt all safety precautions that might be indicated by the activities herein and to avoid all potential hazards. By following the instructions contained herein, the reader willingly assumes all risks in connection with such instructions.

The publisher makes no representation or warranties of any kind, including but not limited to, the warranties of fitness for particular purpose or merchantability, nor are any such representations implied with respect to the material set forth herein, and the publisher takes no responsibility with respect to such material. The publisher shall not be liable for any special, consequential, or exemplary damages resulting, in whole or part, from the readers' use of, or reliance upon, this material.

# CONTENTS

**Introduction Information Sheet**     1

### CHAPTERS 8, 24, 25    Ignition System Service

Information Sheet/Ignition System Service     3
Job Sheet / AT 104-1 Perform a Cylinder Compression Test (Ch.8)     5
Job Sheet / AT 104-2 Perform a Cylinder Leakage Test (Ch. 8)     7
Job Sheet / AT 104-3 Scope Testing an Ignition System (Ch. 24/25)     11
Job Sheet / AT 104-4 Testing an Ignition Coil (Ch. 24/25)     13
Job Sheet / AT 104-5 Individual Component Testing (Ch. 24/25)     15
Job Sheet / AT 104-6 Setting Ignition Timing (Ch. 24/25)     21
Job Sheet / AT 104-7 Visually Inspecting an Electronic Ignition System (Ch. 24/25)     23
Case Study (Ch. 24/25)     24
**Review Questions**     25

### CHAPTERS 33/34    On Board Diagnostic Systems and On Board Diagnostic System Service

Information Sheet/OBD Systems and OBD System Service     27
Job Sheet / AT 104-8 Retrieve Codes from the Computer of an Engine Trouble Control System (Ch. 33/34)     33
Job Sheet / AT 104-9 Test an ECT Sensor (Ch. 33/34)     35
Job Sheet / AT 104-10 Test the Operation of a TP Sensor (Ch. 33/34)     37
Job Sheet / AT 104-11 Test an $O_2$ Sensor (Ch. 33/34)     39
Job Sheet / AT 104-12 Testing a MAP Sensor (Ch. 33/34)     43
Job Sheet / AT 104-13 Conduct a Diagnostic Check on an Engine Equipped with OBD II (Ch.33/34)     47
Job Sheet / AT 104-14 Monitor the Adaptive Fuel Strategy on an OBD II-Equipped Vehicle (Ch. 33/34)     51
Case Studies (Ch. 33/34)     53
**Review Questions**     54

### CHAPTERS 33/34    Diagnosing Engine Performance Problems Using a Chassis Dynamometer

Information Sheet/Diagnosing Engine Performance Problems Using a Chassis Dynamometer     57
Job Sheet / AT 104-15 Analyzing the Horsepower Curve Using the Chassis Dynamometer (Ch. 33/34)     59
Job Sheet / AT 104-16 Diagnosing Performance Problems Using the Chassis Dynamometer (Ch. 33/34)     63

Job Sheet / AT 104-17 Diagnosing Engine Control Sensors Using
the Chassis Dynamometer (Ch. 33/34) 67
**Review Questions** 71
ASE Prep Test 73

# INTRODUCTION INFORMATION SHEET

## DRIVEABILITY DIAGNOSTICS

The ignition, fuel, and emission systems used found on modern automobiles are some of the most advanced systems ever designed. Today's automobile contains more computing power than the Apollo spacecraft used to put our astronauts on the moon. These systems use a network of input and output devices and tie directly into the electronic engine management system. A thorough understanding of these systems is essential for the modern automobile technician to be successful.

Most of the job sheets in this section will familiarize the student with the ignition and engine management systems that are part of the overall engine performance system.

# INFORMATION SHEET

## Ignition System Service

## INFORMATION

The ignition system has many different parts, each with its own purpose. These parts can be categorized by looking at their operating voltages. Those parts that operate by battery voltage are part of the primary ignition circuit. The parts that operate under high voltage (over 25,000 volts) are part of the secondary ignition circuit. This increase in voltage is a result of actions by the ignition coil(s), which has parts of the primary and secondary ignition circuits.

The high voltage of the secondary circuit is what is used to ignite the air/fuel mixture in the engine's combustion chamber.

High voltage is induced in the ignition coil when the magnetic field around the coil's primary winding collapses. As the field collapses, it passes over the secondary windings of the coil and high voltage is induced. The buildup of magnetism around the primary winding is a result of current flow through the winding. The collapsing of the field results from stopping the flow of current.

The primary circuit's responsibility is to control current flow through the primary winding. With the primary circuit, timing is everything. The longer current is allowed to flow through the winding, the more voltage that will be induced into the secondary winding. When the current flow is stopped, ignition begins. An ignition module is responsible for the timing of the primary circuit.

The ignition module may be a separate unit or it may be part of the engine control computer. The module sets the timing based on a program and input from a variety of engine sensors.

The secondary circuit is the pathway for the high voltage from the ignition coil(s) to reach the cylinders. At the end of the voltage path is the spark plug(s). The high voltage jumps across the spark plug gap causing a spark that ignites the air/fuel mixture.

There are two basic types of ignition systems found on today's vehicles: distributor ignition (DI) and distributorless (DIS) or electronic ignition (EI) systems. In a distributor-type ignition system, a mechanical system is used to distribute the spark to the individual spark plugs. In a DIS/EI ignition system, an ignition coil is connected directly to one or two spark plugs. An ignition module controls the timing of the individual coils.

Ignition System Service  **15**

# ☐ JOB SHEET / AT 104–5

## Individual Component Testing

Name _____  Station _____  Date _____

## Objective

Upon completion of this job sheet, you will have demonstrated the ability to test components of the primary and secondary ignition system.

Before beginning this job sheet, review **Chapters 24 and 25** of AUTOMOTIVE TECHNOLOGY for additional information.

You must be able to perform these tasks in order to pass the **ASE** test for: **Engine Performance Certification**

These job sheets meet the requirements for **NATEF** task(s): **Engine Performance**

### Tools and Materials:
AUTOMOTIVE TECHNOLOGY 4e (Thomson, Delmar Learning)
12-volt test light
DMM
Appropriate service manual
Lab scope (DSO)

**NATEF TASKS**
VIII. Engine Performance
Category: C
Task: 1 (P-1)
Task: 2 (P-1)
Task: 3 (P-2)
Task: 4 (P-3)
Task: 5 (P-2)
Task: 6 (P-1)
Task: 8 (P-1)

### Protective Gear:
Goggles or safety glasses with side shields

### Describe the vehicle being worked on:
Year _____ Make _____ Model _____

VIN _____ Engine type and size _____

Type of ignition system _____

Describe general operating condition:

_____

## PROCEDURE

Check the following components:

### Ignition Switch

1. Turn the ignition key off and disconnect the wire connector at the module. ☐ Task completed
2. Disconnect the S terminal of the starter solenoid to prevent the engine from cranking when the ignition is in the run position. ☐ Task completed
3. Turn the key to the run position. ☐ Task completed

4. With the test light, probe the red wire connection to check for voltage. Was there voltage? ___ Yes ___ No
5. Test for voltage at the bat terminal of the ignition coil. Was there voltage? ___ Yes ___ No
6. Turn the key to the start position and check for voltage at the start power wire connector at the module. Was there voltage? ___ Yes ___ No
7. Test for voltage at the bat terminal of the ignition coil. Was there voltage? ___ Yes ___ No

Conclusions:
_____
_____

8. Turn the ignition switch to the off position. ☐ Task completed
9. Install a small straight pin into the appropriate module's input power wire. ☐ Task completed
10. Connect the digital voltmeter's positive lead to the straight pin and ground the negative lead to the distributor base. ☐ Task completed
11. Turn the ignition to the run position. Your voltage reading is _____ volts
12. Turn the ignition to the start position. Your voltage reading is _____ volts

Conclusions:
_____
_____

**Primary Resistor**

1. Turn the ignition off. ☐ Task completed
2. Connect an ohmmeter across the resistor. ☐ Task completed
3. Record your readings: _____ ohms
4. The specified resistance is _____ ohms

Conclusions:
_____
_____

**Pick-Up Coil**

1. Turn the ignition off. ☐ Task completed
2. Remove the distributor cap. ☐ Task completed
3. Connect the ohmmeter to the pick-up coil terminals. ☐ Task completed
4. Record your readings: _____ ohms
5. The specified resistance is _____ ohms

Conclusions:
_____
_____

6. Connect the ohmmeter from one of the pick-up leads to ground. ☐ Task completed
7. Record your readings: _____ ohms
8. The specified resistance is _____ ohms

Conclusions:
_____
_____

9. Reinstall the distributor cap. Then connect the scope leads to the pick-up coil leads. ☐ Task completed
10. Set the scope on its lowest scale. ☐ Task completed
11. Spin the distributor shaft by cranking the engine with the ignition disabled. ☐ Task completed
12. Describe the trace shown on the scope:
_____
_____

Conclusions:
_____
_____

13. Disconnect the scope. ☐ Task completed
14. Connect a voltmeter set on its low voltage scale. ☐ Task completed
15. Describe the meter's action:
_____
_____

Conclusions:
_____
_____

**Hall-Effect Sensors**

1. Connect a 12-volt battery across the plus (+) and minus (–) voltage (supply current) terminals of the Hall layer. ☐ Task completed
2. Connect a voltmeter across the minus (–) and signal voltage terminals. ☐ Task completed
3. Insert a steel feeler gauge or knife blade between the Hall layer and magnet. Then remove the feeler gauge. ☐ Task completed
4. Describe what happens on the voltmeter:
_____
_____

Conclusions:
_____
_____

# 18 Ignition System Service

5. Remove the 12-volt power source and prepare the engine to run.  ☐ Task completed
6. Set a lab scope on its low scale primary pattern position.  ☐ Task completed
7. Connect the primary positive lead to the Hall signal lead; the negative lead should connect to ground or the ground terminal at the sensor's connector.  ☐ Task completed
8. Start the engine and observe the scope.  ☐ Task completed
9. Record the trace on the scope:  ☐ Task completed

_____

_____

Conclusions:

_____

_____

## Control Module

1. Connect one lead of the ohmmeter to the ground terminal at the module and the other lead to a good engine ground.  ☐ Task completed
2. Record your readings: _____ ohms
3. The specified resistance is _____ ohms

Conclusions:

_____

_____

## Secondary Ignition Wires

1. Remove the distributor cap with the spark plug wires attached to the cap but disconnected from the spark plugs.  ☐ Task completed
2. Calibrate an ohmmeter on the X1,000 scale.  ☐ Task completed
3. Connect the ohmmeter leads from the end of a spark plug wire to the distributor cap terminal inside the cap to which the plug wire is connected.  ☐ Task completed
4. Record your readings: _____ ohms
5. The specified resistance is _____ ohms

Conclusions:

_____

_____

## Spark Plugs

1. Remove the engine's spark plugs. Place them on a bench arranged according to the cylinder number.  ☐ Task completed
2. Carefully examine the electrodes and porcelain of each plug.  ☐ Task completed
3. Describe the appearance of each plug:

_____

_____

Conclusions:

_____
_____

4. Measure the gap of each spark plug and record your findings:

_____
_____

5. What is the specified gap? _____ inches

Conclusions:

_____
_____

## Problems Encountered

_____
_____
_____

## Instructor's Comments

_____
_____
_____

Ignition System Service **21**

# ☐ JOB SHEET / AT 104-6

## Setting Ignition Timing

Name _____ Station _____ Date _____

## Objective

Upon completion of this job sheet, you will have demonstrated the ability to check and set the ignition timing on a distributor-type ignition system

Before beginning this job sheet, review **Chapters 24 and 25** of AUTOMOTIVE TECHNOLOGY for additional information.

You must be able to perform these tasks in order to pass the **ASE** test for: **Engine Performance Certification**

These job sheets meet the requirements for **NATEF** task(s): **Engine Performance**

### Tools and Materials:

AUTOMOTIVE TECHNOLOGY 4e (Thomson, Delmar Learning)
Timing light
Tachometer
Appropriate service manual

**NATEF TASKS**
VIII. Engine Performance
Category: C
Task: 7 (P-3)

### Protective Gear:

Goggles or safety glasses with side shields

### Describe the vehicle being worked on:

Year _____ Make _____ Model _____

VIN _____ Engine type and size _____

Describe general operating condition: _____

_____

# PROCEDURE

1. Refer to the service manual or underhood decal and answer the following:

   Ignition Timing Specs _____

   Source of specifications:

   _____

   Conditions that must be met before checking the timing:

   _____

   _____

## 22 Ignition System Service

What should the idle speed be? _____ rpm

What is the idle speed? _____ rpm

If not within specifications, correct the idle before proceeding.  ☐ Task completed

2. Connect the timing light pick-up to the number 1 cylinder's spark plug wire. The power supply wires on the light should be connected to the battery terminals with the proper polarity.  ☐ Task completed

3. Start the engine.  ☐ Task completed

4. The engine must be idling at the manufacturer's recommended rpm, and all other timing procedures must be followed.  ☐ Task completed

5. Aim the timing light marks at the timing indicator and observe the timing marks. Timing found: _____ degrees

6. If the timing mark is not at the specified location, rotate the distributor until the mark is at the specified location. Describe any difficulties you had doing this:

_____

_____

7. Tighten the distributor holddown bolt to the specified torque. What is the specified torque? _____

8. Connect the vacuum advance hose and any other connectors, hoses, or components that were disconnected so that the timing procedure could be done.

## Problems Encountered

_____

_____

_____

## Instructor's Comments

_____

_____

_____

# INFORMATION SHEET

## On Board Diagnostic Systems / On Board Diagnostic System Service

## INFORMATION

Computerized engine control systems present technicians with a totally new way of troubleshooting engine performance problems. On-board diagnostics allow the computer to aid the technician in pinpointing the source of many performance problems.

Until a standardized diagnostic protocol was mandated, there were as many different ways to approach on-board diagnostics as there were vehicle manufacturers. As a result of this mandate, called OBD II, vehicles use the same terms, acronyms, and definitions to describe their components. They also have the same type of diagnostic connector, basic test sequences, and display the same trouble codes. OBD II was gradually phased into production beginning in 1994 and has been on all vehicles sold in North America since 1997.

The three basic subsystems of a computer-control system are the sensors, the PCM, and the actuators. Sensors supply the computer with input on engine conditions. The computer analyzes this data and calculates a response to these conditions. It then signals an output or actuator, such as a relay or solenoid, to adjust engine operation.

All sensors perform the same basic function. They detect a mechanical condition (movement or position), chemical state, or temperature condition and change it into an electrical signal that can be used by the PCM to make decisions.

Outputs and actuators are electromechanical devices that convert an electrical current into mechanical action. This mechanical action can be used to open and close valves, control vacuum to other components, or open and close switches. When the PCM receives an input signal indicating a change in one or more of the operating conditions, the PCM determines the best strategy for handling the condition. The PCM then controls a set of actuators to achieve the desired effect or strategy goal. In order for the computer to control an actuator, it must rely on a component called an output driver. The circuit driver usually applies the ground circuit of the actuator. The ground can be applied steadily if the actuator must be activated for a selected amount of time, or the ground can be pulsed to activate the actuator it pulses.

### SYSTEM OPERATION

Control loops are the cycles by which a process can be controlled by information received from input sensors, ROM, computer processing, and output of specific commands to control actuator devices.
    The basic purpose of all computerized engine control loops is the same: to create an ideal air/fuel ratio which allows the catalytic converter to operate at maximum efficiency while giving the best mileage and performance possible and protecting the engine.

### Diagnostics

When the engine is running, the PCM is receiving inputs from its sensors. The PCM knows the normal range of signals from each sensor in its circuit. If an abnormal signal is received, the PCM notices it.

In most cases, the PCM will simply put this abnormality into its memory and wait for it to occur again. When it does recur, the PCM will illuminate the MIL and store a trouble code in its memory. The code can be retrieved and erased by a technician. Some problems will cause the PCM to immediately store a code and light the MIL. Each manufacturer has slightly different criteria for trouble code setting and MIL lighting. This last statement, however, is not true of OBD II-compliant vehicles.

## Closed Loop Mode

The closed loop mode is basically the same for any automotive system. Sensor inputs are sent to the computer; the computer compares the values to its programs, then sends commands to the output devices. The output devices adjust timing, air/fuel ratio, and emission control operation. The resulting engine operation affects the sensors, which send new messages to the computer, completing the cycle of operation. The complete cycle is called a closed loop.

## Open Loop Mode

When the engine is cold, most electronic engine controls go into open loop mode. In this mode, the control loop is not a complete cycle because the computer does not react to feedback information. Instead, the computer makes decisions based on preprogrammed information that allows it to make basic ignition or air/fuel settings and to disregard sensor inputs. The open loop mode is activated when a signal from the temperature sensor indicates that the engine temperature is too low for gasoline to properly vaporize and burn in the cylinders. Systems with oxygen sensors may also go into the open loop mode while idling, or at any time that the oxygen sensor cools off enough to stop sending a signal and at wide open throttle.

## Fail-Safe or Limp-In Mode

Most computer systems also have what is known as the fail-safe or limp-in mode. The limp-in mode is nothing more than the computer's attempt to take control of vehicle operation when input from one of its critical sensors has been lost. To be more specific, if the computer sees a problem with the signal from a sensor, it either works with fixed values in place of the failed sensor input, or, depending on which input was lost, it can also generate a modified value by combining two or more related sensor inputs.

Some systems have an adaptive learning feature, which makes adjustments to the entire system to compensate for faulty inputs or outputs. In this mode, the driver will have little awareness that there is a problem. Since the engine will run quite well. Depending on the fault identified by the computer, the MIL may not even be lit.

## Computer Logic

In order to control an engine system, the computer makes a series of decisions. Decisions are made in a step-by-step fashion until a conclusion is reached. Generally, the first decision is to determine the engine mode. Then, the computer can choose the best system strategy for the present engine mode. Next, the computer determines the goal to be reached. In a final series of decisions, the computer determines how the goal can be achieved.

## OBD II STANDARDS

OBD II systems were developed in response to the federal government's and the state of California's emission control system monitoring standards for all automotive manufacturers. The main goal of OBD II was to detect when engine or system wear or when component failure caused exhaust emissions to increase by 50 percent or more. OBD II also called for standard service procedures without the use of dedicated special tools.

The OBD II systems must illuminate the MIL if the vehicle conditions would allow emissions to exceed one and a half times the allowable standard for that model year based on a Federal Test Procedure. When a component or strategy failure allows emissions to exceed this level, the MIL is illuminated to inform the driver of a problem, and a diagnostic trouble code is stored in the PCM.

Besides enhancements to the computer's capacities, some additional hardware is required to monitor the emissions performance closely enough to fulfill the tighter constraints and to function beyond merely keeping track of component failures. In most cases, this hardware consists of an additional heated oxygen sensor located down the exhaust stream from the catalytic converter, upgrading specific connectors and components to last the mandated 100,000 miles or 10 years, in some cases a more precise crankshaft or camshaft position sensor (to detect misfires), and a new standardized 16-pin DLC.

## ON-BOARD DIAGNOSTIC SYSTEM DIAGNOSIS AND SERVICE

In the process of controlling the various engine systems, the PCM continuously monitors operating conditions for possible system malfunctions. The computer compares system conditions against programmed parameters. If conditions fall outside the limits of these parameters, the computer detects a malfunction. A trouble code (DTC) is set to indicate the portion of the system that is at fault. A technician can access the code as an aid in troubleshooting.

If a malfunction results in improper system operation, the computer may minimize the effects by using failsafe action. In other words, the computer may substitute a fixed value in place of the real value from a sensor to avoid shutting down the entire system. This fixed value can be programmed into the computer's memory or it can be the last received signal from the sensor prior to failure. This allows the system to operate on a limited basis instead of shutting down completely.

## ELECTRONIC SERVICE PRECAUTIONS

A technician must take some precautions before servicing a computer or its circuit. The PCM is designed to withstand normal current draws associated with normal operation. However, overloading the system will destroy the computer. To prevent damage to the PCM and its related components, follow these service precautions:

1. Never ground or apply voltage to any controlled circuit unless the service manual instructs you to do so.
2. Use only a high-impedance multimeter (10 megaohms or higher) to test the circuits. Never use a test light unless instructed to do so in the manufacturer's suggested procedures.
3. Make sure the ignition switch is turned off before disconnecting or connecting electrical terminals at the PCM.
4. Unless instructed otherwise, turn off the ignition switch before disconnecting or connecting any electrical connections to sensors or actuators.
5. Turn the ignition switch off whenever disconnecting or connecting the battery terminals. Also turn it off when replacing a fuse.
6. Do not connect any electrical accessories to the insulated or ground circuits of computer-controlled systems.
7. Use only manufacturer's specific test and replacement procedures for the year and model of the vehicle being serviced.

### Electrostatic Discharge

Some manufacturers mark certain components and circuits with a code or symbol to warn technicians that they are sensitive to electrostatic discharge. Static electricity can destroy or render a component useless.

When handling any electronic part, especially those that are static sensitive, follow the guidelines below to reduce the possibility of electrostatic buildup on your body and the inadvertent discharge to the electronic part. If you are not sure if a part is sensitive to static, treat it as if it is.

1. Always touch a ground that is known to be good before handling the part. This should be repeated while handling the part and more frequently after sliding across a seat, sitting down from a standing position, or walking a distance.
2. Avoid touching the electrical terminals of the part unless you are instructed to do so in the written service procedures. It is good practice to keep your fingers off all electrical terminals since the oil from your skin can cause corrosion.
3. When you are using a voltmeter, always connect the negative meter lead first.
4. Do not remove a part from its protective package until it is time to install the part.
5. Before removing the part from its package, ground yourself and the package to a ground that is known to be good on the vehicle.

## Basic Diagnosis of Electronic Engine Control Systems

Diagnosing a computer-controlled system is much more than accessing the DTCs in the computer's memory. As is true when diagnosing any system, you need to know what to test, when to test it, and how to test it. Because the capabilities of the engine control computer have evolved from simple to complex, it is important to know the capabilities of the system you are working with before attempting to diagnose a problem. Refer to the service manual for this information. After you understand the system and its capabilities, begin your diagnosis using your knowledge and logic.

Determining which part or area of a computerized engine control system is defective requires a thorough knowledge of how the system works and following a logical troubleshooting process.

Electronic engine control problems are usually caused by defective sensors and, to a lesser extent, output devices. The logical procedure in most cases is, therefore, to check the input sensors and wiring first, then the output devices and their wiring and finally, the computer.

Most late-model computerized engine controls have self-diagnosis capabilities. A malfunction in any sensor, output device, or in the computer itself is stored in the computer's memory as a trouble code. Stored codes can be retrieved and the indicated problem areas checked further.

These methods can be used to check individual system components:

- Visual checks
- Ohmmeter checks
- Voltmeter checks
- Lab scope checks

When diagnosing engine control system problems, service bulletin information is absolutely essential. If a technician does not have service bulletin information, many hours of diagnostic time may be wasted. This information is available from different suppliers of CD-ROMs and paper TSBs.

## SELF-DIAGNOSTIC SYSTEMS

By entering a self-test mode, the computer is able to evaluate the condition of the entire electronic engine control system, including itself. If problems are found, they are identified as either hard faults or intermittent failures. Each type of fault or failure is assigned a numerical trouble code that is stored in computer memory.

A hard fault means a problem has been found somewhere in the system at the time of the self-test. An intermittent problem, on the other hand, indicates a malfunction occurred but is not present at the time of the self-test. Non-volatile RAM allows intermittent faults to be stored for up to a specific number of ignition key on/off cycles. If the trouble does not reappear during that period, it is erased from the computer's memory.

There are various methods of assessing the trouble codes generated by the computer. Most manufacturers have diagnostic equipment designed to monitor and test the electronic components of their vehicles. Aftermarket companies also manufacture scan tools that have the capability to read and record the input and output signals passing to and from the computer.

## OBD II SYSTEM DIAGNOSIS AND SERVICE

OBD II regulations require that the PCM monitor and perform some continuous tests on the engine control system and components. Some OBD II tests are completed at random, at specific intervals, or in response to a detected fault.

To perform the new strategies and tests on the control system, OBD II PCMs have diagnostic management software. The many diagnostic steps and tests required of OBD II systems must be performed under specific operating conditions. The PCM's software organizes and prioritizes the diagnostic routines. The software determines if the conditions for running a test are present. Then it monitors the system for each test and records the results of the tests.

The PCM supplies a buffered low voltage to various sensors and switches. The input and output devices in the PCM include analog to digital converters, signal buffers, counters, and special drivers. The PCM controls most components with electronic switches that complete a ground circuit when turned ON. These switches are arranged in groups of four and seven and are called one of the following: quad driver module or output driver module. The quad driver module can independently control up to four output terminals. The output driver module can independently control up to seven outputs.

The PCM has a learning ability that allows the module to make corrections for minor variations in the fuel system in order to improve driveability. Whenever the battery cable is disconnected, the learning process resets. The driver may note a change in the vehicle's performance. In order to allow the PCM to re-learn, drive the vehicle at part throttle with moderate acceleration.

EEPROM modules are soldered into the PCM. EEPROMs allow the manufacturer to update what is held in the PROM without replacing it. The PCM monitors its internal circuits continuously for integrity. Likewise, it checks its EEPROM for accuracy of its data. It checks its files against what they are supposed to be and sets a code if they are different. Besides the hard-wired memory chip, the PCM also monitors its volatile keep-alive memory. If that has been improperly changed or deleted, the PCM sets a code. This type of code will also be set if the vehicle's battery has been disconnected.

There is a continuous self-diagnosis on certain control functions. This diagnostic capability is complemented by the diagnostic procedures contained in the service manual. The system monitoring diagnostic sequence is a unique segment of the software that is designed to coordinate and prioritize the diagnostic procedures as well as define the protocol for recording and displaying their results.

The diagnostic tables and functional checks given in service manuals are designed to locate a faulty circuit or component through a process of logical decisions. The tables are prepared with the assumption that the vehicle functioned correctly at the time of assembly and that there are not multiple faults present.

## Diagnosis of Computer Voltage Supply and Ground Wires

To operate properly, all PCMs (OBD-II and earlier designs) must have good ground connections and the correct voltage at the required terminals. A wiring diagram for the vehicle being tested must be used for these tests.

Computer ground wires usually extend from the computer to a ground connection on the engine or battery. With the ignition switch on, connect a digital voltmeter from the battery ground to the computer ground. The voltage drop across the ground wires should be 30 millivolts or less. If the voltage reading is greater than that or more than that specified by the manufacturer, repair the ground wires or connection.

Not only should the computer ground be checked, but so should the ground (and positive) connection at the battery. Inspecting the condition of the battery and its cables should always be part of the initial visual inspection that is done before beginning the diagnosis of an engine control system.

A voltage drop test is a quick way of checking the condition of any wire. To do this, connect a voltmeter across the wire or device being tested. Place the positive lead on the most positive side of the circuit. Then turn on the circuit. Ideally there should be a zero volt reading across any wire unless it is a resistance wire that is designed to drop voltage. Even then, check the drop against specifications to see if it is dropping too much.

Poor grounds can also allow EMI or noise to be present on the reference voltage signal. This noise causes small changes in the voltage going to the sensor. Therefore, the output signal from the sensor will also have these voltage changes. The computer will try to respond to these small rapid changes, which can cause a driveability problem. The best way to check for noise is to use a lab scope.

Connect the lab scope between the 5-volt reference signal into the sensor and the ground. The trace on the scope should be flat. If noise is present, move the scope's negative probe to a ground that is known to be good. If the noise disappears, the sensor's ground circuit is bad or has resistance. If the noise is still present, the voltage feed circuit is bad or there is EMI in the circuit from another source, such as the AC generator. Find and repair the cause of the noise.

## Testing Input Sensors

If a DTC directs you to a faulty sensor or sensor circuit or if you suspect that a sensor is faulty, it should be tested. Testing sensors is included here to orient you to the basic procedures. The recommended procedures given in a service manual may differ from those described here. Always follow the manufacturer's recommendations. Sensors are tested with a DMM, scanner, and/or lab scope.

## Testing Actuators

Most computer-controlled actuators are electromechanical devices that convert the output commands from the computer into mechanical action. These actuators are used to open and close switches, control vacuum flow to other components, and operate valves depending on the requirements of the system.

Most systems allow for testing of the actuator through a scan tool. Actuators that are duty cycled by the computer are more accurately diagnosed using this method. Prior to diagnosing an actuator, make sure the engine's compression, ignition system, and intake system are in good condition. Using a scanner, you can use serial data to diagnose outputs. The displayed data should be compared with specifications to determine the condition of any actuator. Also, when an actuator is suspected of being faulty, make sure the inputs related to the control of that actuator are within normal range. Faulty inputs will cause an actuator to appear faulty.

If the actuator is tested by means other than a scanner, always follow the manufacturer's recommended procedures. Because many actuators operate with 5 to 7 volts, never connect a jumper wire from a 12-volt source unless directed to do so by the appropriate service procedure. Some actuators are easily tested with a voltmeter by testing for input voltage to the actuator. If there is the correct amount of input voltage, check the condition of the ground. If both of these are good, then the actuator is faulty. If an ohmmeter needs to be used to measure the resistance of an actuator, disconnect it from the circuit first.

When checking anything with an ohmmeter, logic can dictate good and bad readings. If the meter reads infinite, that means there is an open. Based on what you are measuring across, an open could be good or bad. The same is true for very low resistance readings. Across some things, this would indicate a short. For example, you do not want an infinite reading across the windings of a solenoid. You want low resistance. However, you do want an infinite reading from one winding terminal to the case of the solenoid. If you have low resistance, the winding is shorted to the case.

Most computer-controlled circuits are ground-controlled circuits. The PCM energizes the actuator by providing the ground. On a scope trace, the on-time pulse is the downward pulse. On positive-feed circuits where the computer is supplying the voltage to turn a circuit on, the on-time pulse is the upward pulse. One complete cycle is measured from one on-time pulse to the beginning of the next on-time pulse.

Actuators are electromechanical devices, meaning they are electrical devices that cause some mechanical action. When actuators are faulty, it is because they are electrically faulty or mechanically faulty. By observing the action of an actuator on a lab scope, you will be able to watch its electrical activity. Normally, if there is a mechanical fault, this will affect its electrical activity as well. Therefore, you get a good sense of the actuator's condition by watching it on a lab scope.

# JOB SHEET / AT 104-13

## Conduct a Diagnostic Check on an Engine Equipped with OBD II

Name _____ Station _____ Date _____

## Objective

Upon completion of this job sheet, you will have demonstrated the ability to tconduct a system inspection and retrieve codes from the PCM of an OBD-II-equipped engine.

Before beginning this job sheet, review **Chapters 33 and 34** of AUTOMOTIVE TECHNOLOGY for additional information.

You must be able to perform these tasks in order to pass the **ASE** test for: **Engine Performance Certification**

These job sheets meet the requirements for **NATEF** task(s): **Engine Performance**

### Tools and Materials:
AUTOMOTIVE TECHNOLOGY 4e (Thomson, Delmar Learning)
A vehicle equipped with OBD II
Scan tool
Service manual

**NATEF TASKS**
VIII. Engine Performance
Category: B
Task: 2 (P-1)

### Protective Gear:
Goggles or safety glasses with side shields

### Describe the vehicle being worked on:

Year _____ Make _____ Model _____

VIN _____ Engine type and size _____

Describe general operating condition:

_____

## PROCEDURE

1. Describe the scan tool being used.

   Model _____

2. Inspect all vehicle grounds, including the battery and computer ground, for clean and tight connections. Comments.

   _____

   _____

3. Perform a voltage drop test across all related ground circuits. State where you tested and what your findings were.

   _____

   _____

4. Inspect all vacuum lines and hoses, as well as the tightness of all attaching and mounting bolts in the induction system. Comments.

_____
_____

5. Inspect for damaged air ducts. Comments.

_____
_____

6. Inspect the ignition circuit, especially the secondary cables for signs of deterioration, insulation cracks, corrosion, and looseness. Comments.

_____
_____

7. Are there any unusual noises or odors? If there are, describe them and tell what may be causing them.

_____
_____

8. Inspect all related wiring and connections at the PCM. Comments.

_____
_____

9. Gather all pertinent information about the vehicle and the customer's complaint. This should include detailed information about any symptoms from the customer, a review of the vehicle's service history, published TSBs, and the information in the service manual.

10. Are there any vacuum leaks? ___ Yes ___ No

11. Is the engine's compression normal? ___ Yes ___ No

12. Is the ignition system operating normally? ___ Yes ___ No

13. Are there any obvious problems with the air/fuel system? ___ Yes ___ No

14. Your conclusions from the above.

_____
_____

15. Observe the operation of the MIL by turning the ignition ON. Describe what happened and what it means.

_____
_____

16. Connect the scan tool to the DLC. ☐ Task completed

17. Enter the vehicle identification information into the scan tool. ☐ Task completed

18. Then retrieve the DTCs with the scan tool. ☐ Task completed

19. List all codes retrieved by the scan tool.
    _____
    _____

20. Conclusions from these tests and checks.
    _____
    _____

## Problems Encountered

_____
_____
_____

## Instructor's Comments

_____
_____
_____

# INFORMATION SHEET

## Diagnosing Engine Performance Problems Using a Chassis Dynamometer

### INFORMATION

A chassis dynamometer can be a crucial diagnostic tool when it comes to repairing tough engine performance and drivability problems. The chassis dynamometer can be used to simulate conditions that could not be safely or accurately done during a normal road test when diagnosing drivability problems. It is a critical tool in diagnosing emission control failures that are used in states that require the IM240 emission system test.

While the chassis dynamometer is an outstanding diagnostic tool, special precautions must be taken to ensure it is operated safely. Care must be taken to remove all debris that may have accumulated in the tire tread so it does not become airborne during testing. The vehicle must be securely tied down and the wheels chocked. The operator must be specially trained and familiar with the operating characteristics and safety precautions necessary to run the chassis dynamometer.

# Diagnosing Engine Performance Problems Using a Chassis Dynamometer

## ☐ JOB SHEET / AT 104-15

### Analyzing the Horsepower Curve Using the Chassis Dynamometer

Name _____ Station _____ Date _____

### Objective

Upon completion of this job sheet, you will have demonstrated the ability to understand the desired performance characteristics of an engine by comparing and analyzing the horsepower and rpm graphical data of a test vehicle. You will also be able to identify performance characteristics evident in a vehicle with drivability or performance problems.

Before beginning this job sheet, review **Chapters 33 and 34** of AUTOMOTIVE TECHNOLOGY for additional information.

You must be able to perform these tasks in order to pass the **ASE** test for: **Engine Performance Certification**

These job sheets meet the requirements for **NATEF** task(s): **Engine Performance**

**Tools and Materials:**
AUTOMOTIVE TECHNOLOGY 4e (Thomson, Delmar Learning)
Chassis dynamometer
Basic hand tools
All-Data®

**Protective Gear:**
Safety glasses or goggles
Chassis Dynamometer Operation and Setup Manual

**NATEF TASKS**
VIII. Engine Performance
Category: B
Task: 1 (P-2)
Task: 2 (P-1)
Task: 3 (P-1)
Task: 4 (P-1)
Category: C
Task: 1 (P-1)
Task: 2 (P-1)

**Describe the vehicle being worked on:**
Year _____ Make _____ Model _____
VIN _____ Engine type and size _____

## PROCEDURE

**NOTE:** *A chassis dynamometer can only be operated under strict instructor supervision.*

Describe the general operating condition of the vehicle you will be testing.

_____
_____

1. Using your scan tool, run a DTC analysis on your test vehicle. What codes (if any) exist, and what is the operating condition of the vehicle?

_____
_____

2. For this engine and vehicle, what is the advertised horsepower and torque?

   Horsepower: _____ at _____ rpm

   Torque: _____ at _____ rpm

   Is this specification at the crankshaft or rear wheel? _____

3. Warm up the engine to operating temperature.

   Run the vehicle on the dynamometer in the "Performance Test" mode per the manufacturer's instructions. What are your readings for Maximum Horsepower and Torque?

   HP _____   Torque _____

   What does this indicate as you compare the manufacturer's specifications to your readings?

   _____

   *This has been your "baseline" test. All other tests should be done at the same engine temperature.*

4. After the vehicle has been "faulted" to diminish the vehicle power, as appropriate to your particular test vehicle and under the direction of your instructor, run the vehicle on the dynamometer in the "Performance Test" mode for "Horsepower Curve."

   What are your readings?

   HP _____   Torque _____

   What do the readings indicate? _____

5. Print out the "Vehicle Test Results—Horsepower Curve" graph containing the two test runs. If an on-board printer is not attached, copy results to a floppy disk to print at an available printer.   ☐ Task completed

6. Examine the graph line representing the test with the vehicle "faulted."

   a. What is the maximum HP indicated at the point where the initial upward acceleration levels off and becomes more constant? _____

   b. What is the rpm at this point? _____

   c. At the half-way point where the rpm's are half of the maximum indicated, what is the HP achieved? _____

   d. At the end of the run where the vehicle rapidly decelerates, what is the HP? _____

7. Examine the graph line representing the test vehicle "before" the fault or malfunction was inserted.

   a. What is the maximum HP indicated at the point where the initial upward acceleration levels off and becomes more constant? _____

   b. What is the rpm at this point? _____

c. At the half-way point where the rpm's are half of the maximum indicated, what is the HP achieved? _____

d. At the end of the run where the vehicle rapidly decelerates, what is the HP? _____

8. Compare the two sets of performance characteristics:

   a. What is the difference in HP at the end of initial acceleration? _____

   b. What is the difference in HP at the mid-point of the test run? _____

   c. What is the difference in HP at the end just before deceleration? _____

   d. How many rpm's were necessary to achieve maximum HP with each test run? First Test (unfaulted) _____ Second Test (faulted) _____

9. Remove the fault from the test vehicle, check for any DTCs created, and clear any DTCs.

10. Summarize below what performance characteristics are evident in a properly operating vehicle in comparison to a malfunctioning vehicle where power is affected.

    _____
    _____

11. Explain what the relationship between rpm's and horsepower in a properly operating vehicle in comparison to a malfunctioning vehicle where power is affected.

    _____
    _____

## Problems Encountered

_____
_____
_____

## Instructor's Comments

_____
_____
_____

# ☐ JOB SHEET / AT 104-16

## Diagnosing Performance Problems Using the Chassis Dynamometer

Name _____ Station _____ Date _____

## Objective

Upon completion of this job sheet, you will have demonstrated the ability to determine how simulated faults affecting timing and cylinder balance affect engine performance and drivability.

Before beginning this job sheet, review **Chapters 33 and 34** of AUTOMOTIVE TECHNOLOGY for additional information.

You must be able to perform these tasks in order to pass the **ASE** test for: **Engine Performance Certification**

These job sheets meet the requirements for **NATEF** task(s): **Engine Performance**

### Tools and Materials:
AUTOMOTIVE TECHNOLOGY 4e (Thomson, Delmar Learning)
Chassis dynamometer
Timing light or scan tool
All-data®
Basic hand tools

**NATEF TASKS**
VIII. Engine Performance
Category: B
Task: 1 (P-2)
Task: 2 (P-1)
Task: 3 (P-1)
Task: 4 (P-1)
Category: C
Task: 1 (P-1)
Task: 2 (P-1)

### Protective Gear:
Safety glasses or goggles
Chassis Dynamometer Operation and Setup Manual

### Describe the vehicle being worked on:
Year _____ Make _____ Model _____
VIN _____ Engine type and size _____

## PROCEDURE

**NOTE:** *A chassis dynamometer can only be operated under strict instructor supervision.*

Describe the general operating condition of the vehicle you will be testing.

_____
_____

# Diagnosing Engine Performance Problems Using a Chassis Dynamometer

1. Look up the timing specifications for your test vehicle.

   Required timing is _____ ATDC or _____ BTDC at _____ rpm.

   What conditions (if any) are recommended by the manufacturer for setting timing?

   _____

   _____

2. Check the timing. Timing is set at _____.

3. For this engine and vehicle, what is the advertised horsepower and torque?

   Horsepower: _____ at _____ rpm

   Torque: _____ at _____ rpm

   Is this specification at the crankshaft or rear wheel?

   _____

4. Warm up the engine to operating temperature.

   a. Run the vehicle on the dynamometer in the "Performance Test" mode per the manufacturer's instructions. What are your readings for Maximum Horsepower, Torque, Air-Fuel Ratio, and Exhaust Temperature?

   HP _____    Torque _____

   A/F Ratio _____    EGT _____

   What does this indicate as you compare the manufacturer's specifications to your readings?

   _____

   b. Run the vehicle on the dynamometer in the "Elapsed Time Test" mode per the manufacturer's instructions. What are your readings for the quarter-mile elapsed time and the standing start test to 60 mph?

   1/4 Mile Sprint Elapsed Time _____

   Standing Start Time to 60 mph _____

   *This has been your "baseline" test. All other tests should be done at the same engine temperature.*

5. With the engine cool on one half of the cylinders, increase the spark plug gap by 0.010 in.

   Now run the vehicle on the dynamometer in the two test modes. What are your readings?

   HP _____    Torque _____

   A/F Ratio _____    EGT _____

   1/4 Mile Sprint _____    Standing Start to 60 _____

   What do the readings indicate? _____

6. With the engine cool on the same cylinders, decrease the spark plug gap to 0.010 in. below specification.

   Now run the vehicle on the dynamometer in the two test modes. What are your readings?

   HP _____  Torque _____

   A/F Ratio _____  EGT _____

   1/4 Mile Sprint _____  Standing Start to 60 _____

   What does this indicate? _____

   _____

7. Set spark plug gaps back to required specification. ☐ Task completed

8. Bypass or disconnect the electronic or vacuum advance system. ☐ Task completed

   Now run the vehicle on the dynamometer in the two test modes. What are your readings?

   HP _____  Torque _____

   A/F Ratio _____  EGT _____

   1/4 Mile Sprint _____  Standing Start to 60 _____

   What does this indicate? _____

9. Reconnect the timing control system. ☐ Task completed

10. Disconnect one fuel injector electrical connection (multi-port fuel injected engines only). ☐ Task completed

    Now run the dynamometer in the two test modes. What are your readings?

    HP _____  Torque _____

    A/F Ratio _____  EGT _____

    1/4 Mile Sprint _____  Standing Start to 60 _____

    What does this indicate? _____

11. Summarize below what effect a weak or dead cylinder has on power levels and performance.

    _____

    _____

12. Summarize below what effect incorrect plug gap or worn spark plugs have on power levels and performance.

    _____

    _____

## Problems Encountered

## Instructor's Comments

## ☐ JOB SHEET / AT 104-17

## Diagnosing Engine Control Sensors Using the Chassis Dynamometer

Name _____ Station _____ Date _____

## Objective

Upon completion of this job sheet, you will have demonstrated the ability to determine how simulated faults affecting engine control sensors affect engine performance and drivability.

Before beginning this job sheet, review **Chapters 33 and 34** of AUTOMOTIVE TECHNOLOGY for additional information.

You must be able to perform these tasks in order to pass the **ASE** test for: **Engine Performance Certification**

These job sheets meet the requirements for **NATEF** task(s): **Engine Performance**

### Tools and Materials:
AUTOMOTIVE TECHNOLOGY 4e (Thomson, Delmar Learning)
Chassis dynamometer
Timing light or scan tool
All-Data®
Basic hand tools

**NATEF TASKS**
VIII. Engine Performance
Category: B
Task: 1 (P-2)
Task: 2 (P-1)
Task: 3 (P-1)
Task: 4 (P-1)
Category: C
Task: 1 (P-1)
Task: 2 (P-1)

### Protective Gear:
Safety glasses or goggles
Chassis Dynamometer Operation and Setup Manual

### Describe the vehicle being worked on:
Year _____ Make _____ Model _____
VIN _____ Engine type and size _____

## PROCEDURE

**NOTE:** *A chassis dynamometer can only be operated under strict instructor supervision.*

Describe the general operating condition of the vehicle you will be testing.

_____
_____

1. Utilizing the scan tool, run a DTC analysis on your test vehicle. What codes (if any) exist, and what is the operating condition of the vehicle?

   _____

   _____

2. For this engine and vehicle, what is the advertised horsepower and torque?

   Horsepower: _____ at _____ rpm

   Torque: _____ at _____ rpm

   Is this specification at the crankshaft or rear wheel?

   _____

   _____

3. Warm up the engine to operating temperature.

   a. Run the vehicle on the dynamometer in the "Performance Test" mode per the manufacturer's instructions. What are your readings for Maximum Horsepower, Torque, Air-Fuel Ratio, and Exhaust Temperature?

   HP _____     Torque _____

   A/F Ratio _____     EGT _____

   What does this indicate as you compare the manufacturer's specifications to your readings?

   _____

   b. Run the vehicle on the dynamometer in the "Elapsed Time Test" mode per the manufacturer's instructions. What are your readings for the quarter-mile elapsed time and the standing start test to 60 mph?

   ¼ Mile Sprint Elapsed Time _____

   Standing Start Time to 60 mph _____

   *This has been your "baseline" test. All other tests should be done at the same engine temperature.*

4. Disconnect the wires from the oxygen sensor.  ☐ Task completed

   Now run the vehicle on the dynomometer in the two test modes. What are your readings?

   HP _____     Torque _____

   A/F Ratio _____     EGT _____

   ¼ Mile Sprint _____     Standing Start to 60 _____

   What do the readings indicate? _____

   Reconnect the oxygen sensor wires and clear any DTCs.  ☐ Task completed

# Diagnosing Engine Performance Problems Using a Chassis Dynamometer

5. Unplug the EGR control solenoid electrical connector or vacuum line. Plug the line. ☐ Task completed

   Now run the vehicle on the dynamometer in the two test modes. What are your readings?

   HP _____   Torque _____

   A/F Ratio _____   EGT _____

   ¹/₄ Mile Sprint _____   Standing Start to 60 _____

   What do the readings indicate? _____

   Reconnect the EGR connector or vacuum line and clear any DTCs. ☐ Task completed

6. Disconnect the MAP sensor wire connector or vacuum line. ☐ Task completed

   Now run the vehicle on the dynamometer in the two test modes. What are your readings?

   HP _____   Torque _____

   A/F Ratio _____   EGT _____

   ¹/₄ Mile Sprint _____   Standing Start to 60 _____

   What do the readings indicate? _____

   Reconnect the EGR connector or vacuum line and clear any DTCs. ☐ Task completed

7. Loosen the air duct from the outlet side of the Mass Air Flow Sensor. Create a leakage condition to the degree that the vehicle still runs. ☐ Task completed

   Now run the dynamometer in the two test modes. What are your readings?

   HP _____   Torque _____

   A/F Ratio _____   EGT _____

   ¹/₄ Mile Sprint _____   Standing Start to 60 _____

   What do the readings indicate? _____

   Reconnect the air duct and clear any DTCs. ☐ Task completed

8. Disconnect the Engine Coolant Temperature Sensor. ☐ Task completed

   Now run the dynamometer in the two test modes. What are your readings?

   HP _____   Torque _____

   A/F Ratio _____   EGT _____

   ¹/₄ Mile Sprint _____   Standing Start to 60 _____

   What do the readings indicate? _____

   Reconnect the temperature sensor connector and clear any DTCs. ☐ Task completed

9. Disconnect the Air Temperature Sensor ☐ Task completed

   Now run the dynamometer in the two test modes. What are your readings?

   HP _____     Torque _____

   A/F Ratio _____     EGT _____

   1/4 Mile Sprint _____   Standing Start to 60 _____

   What do the readings indicate? _____

   _____

10. Summarize below what effect malfunctioning, non-functioning, or out-of-spec engine and emissions control sensors have on vehicle power levels and performance.

   _____
   _____
   _____
   _____
   _____
   _____

## Problems Encountered

_____
_____
_____

## Instructor's Comments

_____
_____
_____

# Diagnosing Engine Performance Problems Using a Chassis Dynamometer

 **REVIEW QUESTIONS**

1. What safety precautions must be followed before operating the chassis dynamometer?
   _____
   _____
   _____
   _____

2. True or false? A chassis dynamometer can be used to simulate road conditions that would otherwise be unsafe or impractical to duplicate during a road test. _____

3. Describe what the term "baseline test" refers to.
   _____
   _____

4. What two areas are checked with the chassis dynamometer is put in the "Performance Test" mode?
   _____ and _____

5. Explain what readings you are looking for during the "Elapsed Time" test.
   _____
   _____

6. What effect does incorrect spark plug have on engine power, performance, and emissions levels?
   _____
   _____

7. While discussing ECT sensor diagnosis, Technician A says a defective ECT sensor may cause difficult cold engine starting. Technician B says a defective ECT sensor may cause improper operation of emission control devices. Who is correct?
   a. Technician A            c. Both A and B
   b. Technician B            d. Neither A nor B

8. While discussing the 1/4 Mile Sprint Test, Technician A says that this is an excellent way to diagnose engine misfire on acceleration. Technician B says that the Standing Start to 60 mph is the best way to check for engine misfire on acceleration. Who is correct?
   a. Technician A            c. Both A and B
   b. Technician B            d. Neither A nor B

9. When disconnecting the EGR valve and running the Standing Start to 60 mph test, what engine condition is likely to occur?
   _____
   _____

10. Why is it important to establish a "baseline" when performing tests using the chassis dynamometer?
    _____
    _____